GREEN SEA TURTLES

Michael Molnar

LIFE CYCLES OF MARINE ANIMALS

A+

This edition first published in 2012 in the United States of America by Smart Apple Media.

Smart Apple Media
P.O. Box 3263
Mankato, MN, 56002

First published in 2011 by
MACMILLAN EDUCATION AUSTRALIA PTY LTD
15–19 Claremont St, South Yarra, Australia 3141

Visit our web site at www.macmillan.com.au or go directly to www.macmillanlibrary.com.au

Associated companies and representatives throughout the world.

Copyright text © Michael Molnar 2011

Library of Congress Cataloging-in-Publication Data has been applied for.

Publisher: Carmel Heron
Commissioning Editor: Niki Horin
Managing Editor: Vanessa Lanaway
Editor: Tim Clarke
Proofreader: Paige Amor
Designer: Tanya De Silva
Page layout: Tanya De Silva and Raul Diche
Photo researcher: Sarah Johnson (management: Debbie Gallagher)
Illustrators: Ian Faulkner (**7**, **8**); Simon Scales (**21–25**)
Production Controller: Vanessa Johnson

Manufactured in China by Macmillan Production (Asia) Ltd
Kwun Tong, Kowloon, Hong Kong
Supplier Code: CP January 2011

Acknowledgments
The author and publisher are grateful to the following for permission to reproduce copyright material:

Front cover illustrations by Simon Scales.

Back cover photographs: Shutterstock/Rich Carey (Green Sea Turtle underwater), / idreamphoto (Green Sea Turtle and coral reef).

Photographs courtesy of: Auscape/David Parer Elizabeth Parer-Cook, **27**; Copyright © Brandon Cole. All Rights Reserved, **30** (top); Corbis/Ocean, **28**, /Visuals Unlimited, **5**; Dreamstime/Lilithlita, **9**, /Showface, **30** (bottom), /Vanessagifford, **29**; Getty Images/De Agostini, **4** (top), /Fred Bavendam, **7**; iStockphoto/Ron Masessa, **6**; National Geographic Stock/Bill Curtsinger, **26**; Photolibrary/Doug Perrine, **4** (bottom), /Norbert Probst, **11**; Shutterstock/ale1969, **10** (prawn), /alle, **10** (worm), /holbox, **10** (jellyfish & crab), /Andrey Starostin, **10** (seaweed).

While every care has been taken to trace and acknowledge copyright, the publisher tenders their apologies for any accidental infringement where copyright has proved untraceable. They would be pleased to come to a suitable arrangement with the rightful owner in each case.

Contents

Read the story of one green sea turtle's life cycle in these pages.

Words that are printed in **bold** are explained in the Glossary on page 31.

Life Cycles of Marine Animals

Scientists believe that all life on Earth began in the ocean, hundreds of millions of years ago. Today, thousands of different animal **species** live in and around the ocean. No one knows exactly how many different species of **marine** animals there are—hundreds of new species are discovered every year. Although they share the same saltwater **habitat**, all marine animals grow and change differently over time. Each species has its own unique life cycle.

Life Cycles

All living things have a life cycle. An animal's life cycle begins when it is born and is completed when it has young of its own. During their life cycles, different species grow and change in different ways. Everything an animal does throughout its life cycle happens so that it can survive long enough to **reproduce**. Without this circle of life, all living things would become **extinct**.

The life cycles of marine animals can be as different as the animals themselves.

Green Sea Turtles

Green sea turtles are one of the largest and most common species of marine turtle. Sea turtles have a unique life cycle that takes place on land as well as in the sea. Green sea turtles must survive many dangers if they wish to complete their life cycle and have young of their own.

Sea Turtles Are Reptiles

Green sea turtles are reptiles. This means they are **cold-blooded** and must use the sun to warm themselves. Like other reptiles, sea turtles lay eggs. Sea turtles and most other reptiles do not care for their young after they hatch.

Life on Their Own

Hundreds and thousands of sea turtles hatch from their eggs at the same time. However, from the moment a green sea turtle hatches, it is on its own. Female sea turtles do not care for their young. Most of the young turtles will not survive long enough to complete their life cycle.

Green sea turtle hatchlings have to survive without the care of their mother.

What Do Green Sea Turtles Look Like?

Over millions of years, green sea turtles have **adapted** to life in the ocean. They have a hard streamlined shell and large flippers to help them glide through the water.

hard, thick, scaly skin to protect the turtle from predators and sharp coral reefs

a hard, protective shell that is smooth and streamlined so it does not drag through the water

large front flippers to pull the turtle through the water

large scales called scutes

smaller rear flippers to steer through the water and dig holes in the sand to lay eggs in

Green Flesh

Green sea turtles get their name because of the color of their flesh. To look at, green sea turtles are mostly brown.

VITAL STATISTICS

Size: 4.9 feet (1.5 m) long

Weight: more than 440 pounds (200 kg)

Color: mostly brown, with some green

Living Dinosaurs

Sea turtles have been around since the time of the dinosaurs. This means they have been swimming in the ocean for more than 100 million years!

Length Comparison

Leatherback: 115 inches (300 cm)

Loggerhead: 80 inches (210 cm)

Green: 60 inches (150 cm)

Hawksbill: 40 inches (100 cm)

Flatback: 35 inches (90 cm)

Kemp's ridley: 25 inches (70 cm)

nostrils for breathing when the turtle surfaces for air

good eyesight when they are underwater, but poor when out of the water

a gland behind the eyes for getting rid of any extra salt in the turtle's body

a strong, sharp beak for biting off chunks of algae and seagrass

a stretchable neck for reaching into holes in reefs, to look for food

Where Do Green Sea Turtles Live?

Green sea turtles can be found in warm water oceans and seas around the world. During their life cycles, they will live in many different **habitats**. Green sea turtles can be found close to shore, far out to sea and even on land.

Green sea turtles return to the same beaches they hatched from to lay their eggs.

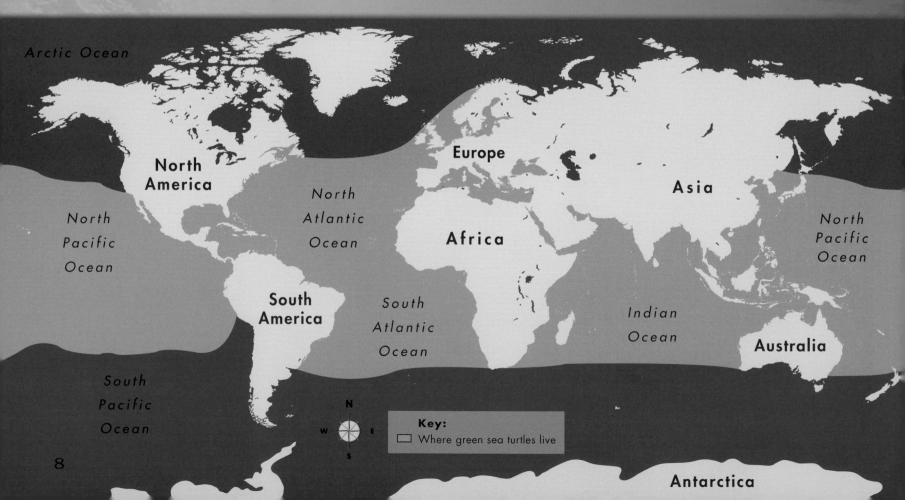

Arctic Ocean

North America

North Pacific Ocean

North Atlantic Ocean

Europe

Asia

North Pacific Ocean

Africa

South America

South Atlantic Ocean

Indian Ocean

South Pacific Ocean

Australia

Key:
☐ Where green sea turtles live

N W E S

Antarctica

Habitats

Green sea turtles live in a variety of habitats, such as coastal bays, reefs, harbors, lagoons, and large saltwater rivers. Young green sea turtles live in the open ocean. Older green sea turtles prefer shallow water, so they are mostly found closer to shore. All green sea turtles like to live around seagrass beds and coral reefs, where they can find lots of food.

Migration

When it is time for green sea turtles to **breed**, they may **migrate** thousands of miles to **mate** and lay eggs. Female turtles find their way back to the beach where they were born. Male green sea turtles follow the females on their migration.

Green sea turtles live in places where they can find food easily.

What Do Green Sea Turtles Eat?

Green sea turtles eat different foods at different stages of their lives. The diet of a young green sea turtle is very different to that of an adult green sea turtle.

Foods That Young Green Sea Turtles Eat

Jellyfish

Seaweed

Crabs

Shrimp

Worms

Sea Grass

Sea grass provides food and shelter for many marine animals. Small fish, shrimp, and crabs depend on seagrass to survive.

Food for Young Green Sea Turtles

Young green sea turtles are omnivorous, which means that they eat both plants and animals. They will try to eat just about anything they can fit in their mouths, including jellyfish, small **crustaceans**, and **marine** plants.

Food for Adult Green Sea Turtles

Adult green sea turtles are herbivores, which means that they mainly eat marine plants, such as sea grass and algae. They can spend much of their day on the sea floor, grazing on sea grass. They use their strong beaks to scrape algae from rocks and reefs.

Green sea turtles hold their breath as they graze on sea grass on the sea floor.

11

THE LIFE CYCLE OF A
GREEN SEA TURTLE

The life cycle of a green sea turtle is full of danger. Only about 1 in every 50 turtles survives long enough to have young and complete their life cycle. Most green sea turtles do not survive more than a few days.

1

A Green Sea Turtle Hatches

Green sea turtles hatch from eggs buried in the sand. Hundreds of turtles hatch at the same time. The young turtles, called hatchlings, spend weeks digging their way out. When they reach the surface, they make their way to the ocean. Once in the water they swim out to sea, where they drift in the currents looking for food.

5

Laying Eggs

A short time after mating, the female turtle drags herself up the same beach she hatched from. Here she digs a hole in the sand and lays her eggs. Two months later the eggs will hatch and her life cycle will be complete.

2 Growing Up at Sea

Green sea turtles spend the first years of their life at sea without their mothers to feed and protect them. They must find their own food and look after themselves. Green sea turtles stay out at sea until they grow to around 12 inches (30 cm) long. This takes about five years.

3 Life Closer to Shore

As green sea turtles grow, they become herbivores. This means that they spend their days feeding on marine plants. Adult sea turtles can grow to more than 440 pounds (200 kg). Green sea turtles are able to breed and lay eggs at around 25 years of age.

4 Migration and Mating

Male sea turtles will fight each other to mate with a female. The winner will mate with the female and she will become **pregnant**. Hundreds of eggs inside her body are **fertilized** and the baby turtles start to grow.

13

Buried in the sand, a baby green sea turtle hatches from her egg. Other baby turtles hatch all around her. They dig at the sand above and slowly make their way to the surface. Just before the turtles break out of the sand, they stop.

The sun is out and it would be much too dangerous for them above ground. They must wait until night before they can make their way to the ocean.

When night falls, the hatchlings emerge from the sand. Together they scramble across the beach to the ocean. Many of the other hatchlings are eaten by crabs and seabirds. The young turtle is lucky and makes it to the water.

Safety in Numbers

Thousands of turtle hatchlings dig their way out of the sand at the same time. There are so many hatchlings that the **predators** cannot eat them all.

The young turtle starts to
swim out to sea.

Hungry fish and sharks surround her, grabbing other young
turtles and swallowing them whole.
Hidden by the darkness, she slips past
the predators and makes it to the open ocean.

After **three days of swimming**, the young turtle is tired. She finds a large patch of floating seaweed and sleeps on its surface.

The seaweed is home to many animals and will provide the young turtle with a lot of food. It will also hide her from predators in the water below as she sleeps.

Sleeping at the Surface

When they sleep, young sea turtles float at the surface of the water so they can breathe.

When the young turtle wakes, she finds the seaweed covered in small crustaceans and **invertebrates**. She greedily munches on anything she can catch. Worms, crabs, and shrimp are all part of her diet. She also chews on the seaweed itself.

For the next six years she drifts with the current, feeding on anything that crosses her path. Even the stinging tentacles of a jellyfish are food for the young turtle.

18

After six years she has grown to around 12 inches (30 cm) long. Bigger and stronger, she can now swim closer to shore to find new feeding grounds.

In the shallows close to shore, she uses her sharp beak to feed on a large patch of seagrass. From now on she will feed mainly on marine plants. Every 20 minutes she returns to the surface to breathe. It is when she is at the surface that she in most in danger.

Sleeping With the Fishes

Adult sea turtles can hold their breath for hours as they sleep on the sea floor.

19

One morning, as the turtle surfaces for air, something grabs hold of her flipper. Suddenly, she is pulled under the water—a tiger shark has her! The shark shakes its head, its sharp teeth tearing off a chunk of her flipper. She tries to escape but she is too slow.

The shark tries to grab the turtle again, but its teeth cannot grab hold of her hard shell. Using her shell as a shield, she swims to shallower water where the tiger shark cannot follow her.

She is missing part of her flipper and her shell is scratched, but she is alive. The ocean can be a dangerous place for a young green sea turtle.

Years later, the turtle's wounds have healed. She is 25 years old and has grown to 220 pounds (100 kg). She is now ready to mate and lay eggs.

She migrates hundreds of miles to the beach where she hatched from her egg. Hundreds of other female turtles have made the same journey. Male sea turtles follow and are ready to mate.

Finding Their Way Home

Many scientists believe that green sea turtles can detect Earth's magnetic field, and use this to find their way back to their nesting beaches.

A mature male swims up behind the female turtle.

Wrapping his flippers around her, he holds onto her shell. The male turtle uses his long tail to **fertilize her eggs.** The two turtles float at the surface of the water as they mate.

A week later, it is **time for the female to lay her eggs.**

Under the cover of night, the green sea turtle makes her way onto the beach. She drags herself up onto the sand.

Once she reaches the dry sand at the top of the beach, she uses her flippers to dig a hole. In the hole she lays more than 100 leathery skinned eggs.

After laying the eggs she covers them with sand and drags herself back to the ocean. Her job as a mother is done. She will not be around to look after the hatchlings. Two months later, the eggs hatch and her life cycle is complete.

The hatchlings dig their way out of the sand and make their way to the ocean. Many years from now, the survivors will return to the same beach and continue this cycle of life.

Male or Female?

The temperature of the nest determines the sex of the turtle hatchlings. If they are kept warm they will all be females. If the eggs are cooler they will all be male.

Large birds such as vultures can swallow small turtles whole.

Threats to the Survival of Green Sea Turtles

Green sea turtles face many dangers during their life cycle. Out of every 100 eggs, only one or two turtles will survive to become adults. Most hatchlings do not survive the first few days of their life. Some dangers are natural and some are caused by humans.

Land Predators

The most dangerous time in a turtle's life is just after it has hatched. Turtle hatchlings are **prey** for many land predators. When the hatchlings dig themselves from the sand they have to make their way across the open beach to the ocean. Many birds, crabs, foxes, and lizards will feed on as many of the turtles as they can.

Marine Predators

Once young turtles make it to the ocean, marine predators lie in wait. Large fish, sharks, and seabirds all feed on young turtles. Green sea turtles that survive long enough to grow larger are safe from most predators. They have a hard shell that most animals cannot bite through.

Tiger Sharks

Tiger sharks are one of just a few animals that can eat large sea turtles. They have strong, sharp, serrated teeth that can saw through a turtle's hard shell if the shark can get a strong grip.

Human Threats to Green Sea Turtles

Many green sea turtles are killed or injured by humans every year. People are also destroying the habitats where turtles feed and lay their eggs. Without food and places to lay their eggs, turtles will not be able to complete their life cycles.

Fishing

Every year, thousands of green sea turtles become tangled in fishing nets and drown. Often fishers are trying to catch other animals and throw the dead turtles back into the ocean. Green sea turtles can also become tangled in discarded nets and lines. These nets can keep killing turtles for many years if they are left in the ocean.

Turtles that become tangled in nets find it hard to swim to the surface to breathe.

Building on the Beach

People like to live near the beach, but this is where green sea turtles lay their eggs. If there are too many people on a beach, turtles will not come ashore to lay their eggs. If they cannot lay their eggs, they cannot complete their life cycle. Young hatchlings can also be confused by bright streetlights and lights from buildings, and get lost on their way to the ocean. If they do not find the ocean they soon die.

Pollution

Pollution can kill and injure sea turtles. They can become tangled in old ropes and fishing lines, causing injuries. Turtles also mistake rubbish for food. A floating plastic bag may look like a jellyfish to a sea turtle. When a turtle eats a plastic bag it can become stuck in its stomach. This can cause the turtle to starve to death.

Beaches are very important in the life cycles of green sea turtles. If beaches are bright and busy with human activity, turtles may not come ashore to lay their eggs.

How Can You Help Protect Green Sea Turtles?

To protect any animal, you must protect its habitat. As well as not harming green sea turtles, people must protect the oceans where turtles live and breed. Only then will the turtles be able to survive and continue their life cycles.

Organizations that protect green sea turtles mark the nests on busy beaches so that the young are not disturbed.

Protect Our Oceans

Protecting our oceans is important for all creatures on Earth, including humans. People get a lot of their food from the ocean. If we destroy and pollute the ocean, people and turtles will not survive. You can help protect our oceans from pollution by putting your rubbish in a bin. This will keep it from blowing into the ocean, where it can cause so much harm.

Join a Group

Many organizations have been set up to try and protect green sea turtles and other marine creatures. If people support these groups, there is a better chance that these animals and our oceans can be saved.

Tell a Friend!

Share your love of green sea turtles with someone else and show them how special sea turtles really are. The more that people know and care about turtles, the more they will want to help.

Glossary

breed	produce young
cold-blooded	to have a body temperature that changes based on the temperature of the surroundings
crustaceans	animals that have their skeleton on the outside of their body, such as crabs and shrimp
extinct	a species that is no longer alive on the planet
fertilized	ready to begin developing into a new young animal
habitat	place where animals, plants, or other living things live
invertebrates	animals without a backbone
marine	related to the oceans or seas
mate	when a male and female come together to produce young
migrate	travel a long distance from one place to another
pollution	waste that harms the environment
predators	animals that eat other animals
pregnant	has young developing inside
prey	animals that are eaten by other animals
reproduce	have young
species	groups of animals or plants with similar features
unique	one of a kind

Index